How to Reach Your Favorite Sports Star 4

▼▼▼▼▼

How to Reach Your Favorite Sports Star 4

▼▼▼▼▼

Dylan B. Tomlinson

LOWELL HOUSE JUVENILE

LOS ANGELES

NTC/Contemporary Publishing Group

For Ashley, we all miss you . . .

Published by Lowell House
A division of NTC/Contemporary Publishing Group, Inc.
4255 West Touhy Avenue, Lincolnwood (Chicago),
Illinois 60646-1975, U.S.A.

Managing Director and Publisher: Jack Artenstein
Director of Publishing Services: Rena Copperman
Editorial Director, Juvenile: Brenda Pope-Ostrow
Director of Juvenile Development: Amy Downing
Director of Art Production: Bret Perry
Typesetter: Justin Segal
Project Editor: Dianne J. Woo

Library of Congress Catalog Card Number: 98-67234

ISBN: 1-56565-702-0

Lowell House books can be purchased at special discounts
when ordered in bulk for premiums and special sales.
Contact Customer Service at the above address,
or call 1-800-323-4900.

Printed and bound in the United States of America

10 9 8 7 6 5 4 3 2

Contents

Reach out and touch your favorite sports star!

*I*f you've ever had the impulse to tell a special sports celeb exactly how you feel, grab a pen and do it now! But how do you reach your favorite sports stars? It's easy. Read about them in the following pages, then write to the address that accompanies each entry. For best results, remember the following:

➤ Don't obsess about spelling, grammar, and/or sounding foolish. These are fan letters you're writing, not English compositions. Remember to have fun!

➤ If you want a reply, it's best to send a self-addressed, stamped envelope (SASE) along with your letter. That's an envelope with a first-class postage stamp and your name and address printed legibly on it.

➤ If you are writing to or from a country other than the United States (for instance, if you are in Canada writing to a star at a U.S. address), you will need to include international postage coupons with your letter. You can purchase international postage coupons at any post office.

➤ Sports stars change addresses and teams just like anybody else. But even if the person you write to is long gone, your letter should be forwarded to his or her new address.

Jennifer Azzi
Point Guard, San Jose Lasers

□ □ □ □ □ □ □ □ □ □ □ □ □ □ □ □ □ □ □

Since 1990, Azzi has been considered one of the top women's basketball players in the world. She led Stanford University to an NCAA Championship in 1990, and helped the U.S. team win a bronze medal in the 1992 Olympics and a gold in the 1996 Olympics. As a member of the Lasers, Azzi is a two-time all-star and one of the best point guards in the American Basketball League (ABL).

Birthday Beat
August 31, 1968

8

□ □ □ □ □ □ □ □ □ □ □ □ □ □ □ □ □ □ □

So You Want to Know—

How Jennifer stays busy when she's not playing basketball? In addition to doing commercials for Reebok and the ABL, Azzi was selected—along with Mets catcher Mike Piazza and soccer superstar Mia Hamm—to be a spokesperson for Pert Plus shampoo, and she's even done some modeling.

Cool Credits

➤ NCAA all-American at Stanford, 1988–90
➤ NCAA Player of the Year, 1990
➤ U.S. National Team, 1990–98
➤ Played in Europe, 1991–95
➤ Led U.S. to Olympic gold medal, 1996
➤ Picked by the Lasers in the first round of the 1996 elite draft

➤ ABL all-star, 1997, 1998
➤ First team all-ABL, 1998

Vital Stats

➤ Height: 5'7"
➤ Weight: 120
➤ Birthplace: Oak Ridge, Tennessee
➤ Current residence: Palo Alto, California
➤ Favorite sport: baseball

• •

Jennifer Azzi
c/o San Jose Lasers
1530 Parkmoor Ave., Suite A
San Jose, CA 95128

• •

Vin Baker
Forward, Seattle Supersonics

▼▼▼▼▼▼▼▼▼▼▼▼▼▼▼▼▼

Cool Credits

➤ NCAA all-American at Hartford College, 1992, 1993
➤ Selected by the Milwaukee Bucks with the No. 8 pick in the 1993 NBA draft
➤ NBA all-star, 1995–98
➤ All-Rookie Team, 1994
➤ All-NBA Third Team, 1997
➤ All-NBA Second Team, 1998

Vital Stats

➤ Height: 6'11"
➤ Weight: 245
➤ Birthplace: Lake Wales, Florida
➤ Current residence: Seattle, Washington
➤ Hobbies: video games and cooking
➤ Favorite food: steak
➤ Favorite actor: Denzel Washington

Birthday Beat
November 23, 1971

So You Want to Know—
How big of a video game fan Baker is? It's his favorite hobby! When he first heard he had been traded to the Supersonics, he had to fly to Seattle immediately to meet his new team-mates and coach. What was the only thing Vin brought with him? His Sega and all of his games, so he could play them in his hotel room.

After playing basketball at Hartford College and for the Milwaukee Bucks, Baker was often referred to as the most underrated player in the NBA. In 1997, when he was traded to the Supersonics, fans finally began to take notice as Baker emerged as one of the best players in the NBA. That was no surprise to any of his fellow players, who always knew he had talent!

Vin Baker
c/o Seattle Supersonics
190 Queen Anne Ave. North,
Suite 200
Seattle, WA 98109-9711

Craig Biggio
Second Baseman, Houston Astros

■ ■ ■ ■ ■ ■ ■ ■ ■ ■ ■ ■ ■ ■ ■ ■

*I*f someone referred to Biggio as the best second baseman in the major leagues, not many would argue. With his ability to get hits, steal bases, and produce runs as well as any of the greats in the game, Biggio has been one of the fastest, most versatile players during his 10 seasons in the pros. Even with power hitters such as Moises Alou and Jeff Bagwell in the lineup, Biggio is a tremendous asset to the Astros.

■ ■ ■ ■ ■ ■ ■ ■ ■ ■ ■ ■ ■ ■ ■

So You Want to Know—

How Craig spends his free time? When he's not with his wife and two young sons, Conor and Cavan, he donates his time to the Sunshine Kids, a support organization for children who have cancer. In 1991, Biggio was given the Bart Giamatti Caring Award, in recognition of his community and charity work.

Cool Credits

➤ NCAA all-American at Seton Hall, 1987
➤ Selected by the Astros in the first round of the 1987 baseball draft
➤ Major-league all-star, 1989, 1991–97
➤ Won the Gold Glove as best fielder in his position, 1994–97
➤ Led the league in runs scored with 146, 1997

Vital Stats

➤ Height: 5'11"
➤ Weight: 180
➤ Birthplace: Smithtown, New York
➤ Current residence: Spring Lake, New Jersey

Birthday Beat
December 14, 1965

Craig Biggio
c/o Houston Astros
P.O. Box 288
Houston, TX 77001-0288

Debbie Black

Point Guard, Colorado Xplosion

□ □ □ □ □ □ □ □ □ □ □ □ □ □ □ □ □ □

*A*ll her life, people have been telling Black that she's too short to play basketball. Fortunately, she never listened. Now she's one of the quickest players and best defenders in the American Basketball League (ABL). Known for her scrappy play, the 5' 3" Black frequently snatches rebounds away from players who are more than a foot taller than her. Debbie won't hesitate to jump into the stands to keep a ball from going out of bounds, dive across the floor for a loose ball, and literally drive all of her opponents nuts!

So You Want to Know—

What Black plans to do when her playing career is over? Although Debbie has no plans to retire anytime soon, when she does, she would like to become a coach. Anybody who has ever watched her play knows she would be a natural!

Vital Stats

➤ Height: 5'3"
➤ Weight: 110
➤ Birthplace: Philadelphia, Pennsylvania
➤ Current residence: Philadelphia, Pennsylvania
➤ Nickname: The Tasmanian Devil

14

Cool Credits

➤ Graduated from St. Joseph's University, 1988

➤ Played professional basketball in Australia, 1988–96

➤ Member of the 1997 USA National Invitational Team

➤ ABL Defensive Player of the Year, 1997

➤ Led ABL in steals with 4.1 per game, 1997

➤ Had first ever quadruple double in women's basketball history with 10 points, 14 rebounds, 12 assists, and 10 steals against the Atlanta Glory in 1997

➤ ABL all-star, 1997, 1998

➤ Xplosion team captain, 1997, 1998

Birthday Beat

July 29, 1966

Debbie Black
c/o Colorado Xplosion
800 Grant St.
Denver, CO 80203

Kobe Bryant

Shooting Guard, Los Angeles Lakers

▼▼▼▼▼▼▼▼▼▼▼▼▼▼▼▼▼▼▼▼

Bryant has always been ready to face any challenge. After being named High School Player of the Year in 1996, he decided to take his game to the highest level, the NBA. It didn't take Kobe long to adjust, and he soon succeeded. Despite being the league's youngest player, he was immediately able to contribute to the Los Angeles Lakers. Bryant was a second team all-rookie selection and won the NBA Slam Dunk Contest. During his second season, he started for the Western Conference in the NBA All-Star Game, proving that age is not a factor for someone with his talent and drive.

Cool Credits

➤ Named High School Player of the Year, 1996
➤ Selected by the Charlotte Hornets with the 13th pick in the NBA draft, 1996

Birthday Beat

August 23, 1978

So You Want to Know—

Why Bryant is so popular in Europe? Probably because Europeans were the first to see him play. Kobe, who speaks fluent Italian, started playing basketball at the age of 5, when his father was playing the game professionally in Italy. In a poll, Italians ranked Bryant as the most popular player in the country, even ahead of Michael Jordan. Not bad for a 19-year-old!

➤ Traded to the Lakers for Vlade Divac, 1996
➤ Won the NBA Slam Dunk Contest, 1997
➤ NBA All-Rookie Second Team, 1997
➤ Was the youngest player ever to start an NBA game, against the Minnesota Timberwolves, November 3, 1997
➤ NBA all-star, 1998

Vital Stats
➤ Height: 6'7"
➤ Weight: 210
➤ Birthplace: Philadelphia, Pennsylvania
➤ Current residence: Los Angeles, California
➤ Favorite music: rap
➤ Romance update: is dating singer/actress Brandy

Kobe Bryant
c/o Los Angeles Lakers
3900 W. Manchester Blvd.
P.O. Box 10
Inglewood, CA 90305-2227

Terrell Davis

Running Back, Denver Broncos

■ ■ ■ ■ ■ ■ ■ ■ ■ ■ ■ ■ ■ ■ ■ ■

Vital Stats

➤ Height: 5'11"
➤ Weight: 200
➤ Birthplace: San Diego, California
➤ Current residence: Aurora, Colorado
➤ Hobby: playing Sega (John Madden Football is his favorite)

Cool Credits

➤ NFL All-Rookie Team, 1995
➤ Offensive Player of the Year, 1996
➤ NFL all-pro, 1996, 1997
➤ NFL Pro Bowl, 1997, 1998
➤ *Pro Football Weekly* Player of the Year, 1997
➤ Super Bowl MVP, 1998

So You Want to Know—

What Davis did after winning the Super Bowl MVP in 1998? He headed to where any other MVP would go . . . the talk show circuit. Terrell appeared on the *Tonight Show with Jay Leno*, *The Late Show with David Letterman*, and *Politically Incorrect*. Somewhere along the way Davis caught the acting bug and has appeared on the TV show *Moesha* and HBO's *Arli$$*.

Birthday Beat

October 28, 1972

For more than 20 years, "Broncos" and "Super Bowl" could not be mentioned in the same sentence without generating a few laughs. Denver always seemed to come up short in the Super Bowl. All that changed in 1998 when the Broncos were victorious at last, thanks in part to Davis, one of the best running backs in the game. In 1995, Davis was an unknown from the University of Georgia, but he soon proved himself by rushing for more than 1,000 yards each season. Now Terrell is one of the most feared running backs in the NFL, and the Broncos are the best team. It's probably not a coincidence!

Terrell Davis
c/o Denver Broncos
13655 Broncos Parkway
Englewood, CO 80112

Tim Duncan

Power Forward, San Antonio Spurs

□ □ □ □ □ □ □ □ □ □ □ □ □ □ □ □ □ □ □

*A*fter getting Duncan with the first pick in the 1997 NBA draft, the Spurs went from being the third worst team in the league in 1996–97 to being in the playoffs in 1997–98. As a rookie, Tim averaged more than 20 points and 10 rebounds a game, a feat that was last accomplished by Shaquille O'Neal in 1992. With David Robinson and Duncan in the lineup, San Antonio has its own twin towers. No wonder the Spurs were one of the hottest teams in the NBA in 1997–98.

So You Want to Know—

If Duncan has always been a basketball star? Amazingly, the answer is no. Duncan didn't begin playing basketball until his junior year in high school. Before that, his best sport was swimming. He was so good at it he almost got to represent the Virgin Islands at the 1988 Olympics.

Birthday Beat
April 25, 1976

20

Cool Credits

➤ Earned a degree in psychology from Wake Forest University
➤ NCAA Player of the Year, 1997
➤ NCAA all-American, 1995–97
➤ First pick in the 1997 NBA draft
➤ NBA Rookie of the Year, 1998
➤ Only rookie to play in the All-Star Game, 1998

Vital Stats

➤ Height: 7'
➤ Weight: 248
➤ Birthplace: St. Croix, U.S. Virgin Islands
➤ Current residence: San Antonio, Texas
➤ Favorite movie: *The Crow*
➤ Favorite music: reggae

Tim Duncan
c/o San Antonio Spurs
100 Montana St.
San Antonio, TX 78203-1031

Warrick Dunn

Running Back, Tampa Bay Buccaneers

▼▼▼▼▼▼▼▼▼▼▼▼▼▼▼▼▼▼▼▼▼▼▼▼

When Dunn came out of Florida State University in 1997, team after team said, "He's too small." Warrick didn't care. After he had played only a few games, coaches and fans alike were saying, "He's too fast." Dunn was the league's most dominant rookie in 1997 as he led Tampa Bay to its first playoff appearance in more than a decade. With his mobility and breakaway speed, Dunn quickly established himself as one of the best young runners in the NFL.

Birthday Beat
January 5, 1975

Cool Credits

➤ NCAA all-American at Florida State, 1995, 1996
➤ Selected by the Buccaneers with the 12th pick in the NFL draft, 1997
➤ Rookie of the Year, 1997
➤ NFL all-pro, 1997

Vital Stats

➤ Height: 5'8"
➤ Weight: 176
➤ Birthplace: Baton Rouge, Louisiana
➤ Current residence: Tallahassee, Florida
➤ Favorite food: Cajun
➤ Favorite TV show: ESPN's *SportsCenter*

So You Want to Know—

If Dunn keeps his promises? You better believe he does. Before his mother died, he promised her that he would finish his degree at Florida State. Dunn turned down millions of dollars from the NFL to return to Florida State for his senior year. He graduated with a degree in information studies in May 1997.

Warrick Davis
c/o Tampa Bay Buccaneers
One Buccaneer Place
Tampa, FL 33607

Jeff Gordon

Race Car Driver

I t didn't take Gordon long to make his presence felt on the 1995 Winston Cup Tour. At the age of 24, Gordon became the youngest points champion of the modern era. At the age of 5, when most kids are just starting kindergarten, Jeff was already racing. In 1979, 8-year-old Gordon was the Quarter-Midget National Champion. He hasn't slowed down since and continues to be one of the top race car drivers in the world—not to mention one of the most popular!

Vital Stats

➤ Height: 5'7"
➤ Weight: 150
➤ Birthplace: Pittsboro, Indiana
➤ Hobbies: water skiing, snow skiing, racquetball, and video games
➤ Family ties: a wife, Brooke

Cool Credits

➤ Won Midget Championship, 1990
➤ Winston Cup Rookie of the Year, 1993
➤ Won Coca-400 and Brickyard 400, 1994
➤ American Driver of the Year, 1995
➤ Won NASCAR points title, 1995, 1996, 1997
➤ Won Daytona 500, 1997

So You Want to Know—

What Jeff thinks is the key to all his wins on the racing circuit? His car and his racing team, the Rainbow Warriors, deserve some of the credit, but Gordon is also incredibly superstitious. He doesn't allow anyone on his team to wear green, and he won't let anyone on his team eat peanuts because he thinks they're bad luck.

Jeff Gordon
c/o Harris Group
P.O. Box 515
514 E. Route 66
Williams, AZ 86046
http://www.JeffGordonfanclub.com

Cammi Granato

1998 Olympic Women's Hockey Team

So You Want to Know—

If it was a Granato family affair at the Olympics in Nagano, Japan? You'd better believe it. With brother Tony playing for the men's team and Cammi playing for the women's team, the Granatos had virtually every friend and relative at their side in Japan. Cammi fared much better than her older brother, whose team was knocked out in the semifinals, but no one was more proud of Cammi than Tony when his sister brought home the gold medal.

Cool Credits

➤ NCAA all-American at Providence College, 1990–93
➤ Member of the U.S. National Team, 1990, 1992, 1994–98
➤ USA Hockey Player of the Year, 1996
➤ Led U.S. to Olympic gold medal, 1998

Vital Stats

➤ Height: 5'7"
➤ Weight: 140
➤ Birthplace: Maywood, Illinois
➤ Current residence: Downers Grove, Illinois
➤ Favorite team: Chicago Blackhawks

Birthday Beat
March 25, 1971

*I*n 1998, Granato finally stopped being referred to as the little sister of Tony Granato, who plays for the NHL's San Jose Sharks. Cammi proved she was capable of playing a little hockey herself when she helped lead the United States to the first gold medal ever in women's hockey at the 1998 Olympics. With the possibility of a women's professional league now on the horizon, Cammi should be able to keep pace with her older brother.

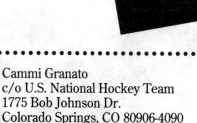

Cammi Granato
c/o U.S. National Hockey Team
1775 Bob Johnson Dr.
Colorado Springs, CO 80906-4090

Ken Griffey Jr.

Outfielder, Seattle Mariners

▼▼▼▼▼▼▼▼▼▼▼▼▼▼▼▼▼▼

Cool Credits

➤ Selected by the Mariners with the first pick in the 1987 major-league draft
➤ Major-league all-star, 1990–97
➤ Won eight Gold Gloves, 1990–97
➤ Led American League in home runs, 1994, 1997
➤ Led American League in RBIs, 1997
➤ American League MVP, 1997
➤ Second youngest player to reach 300 home runs, 1998

Vital Stats

➤ Height: 6'3"
➤ Weight: 205
➤ Birthplace: Donora, Pennsylvania
➤ Current residence: Issaquah, Washington
➤ Hobby: playing Sega
➤ Family ties: a wife, Melissa, and a 4-year-old son, Trey

Birthday Beat

November 21, 1969

▼▼▼▼▼▼▼▼▼▼▼▼▼▼▼▼▼▼▼▼

When Griffey steps into the batting box for the Mariners, opposing pitchers know they're in for a tough time. Griffey has consistently been the best power hitter in the American League since joining the big leagues in 1989. Ken has hit more than 40 home runs four times in his young career. In 1997, he almost broke the major-league record of 61 home runs when he blasted 56 homers, the most in the American League since 1961.

So You Want to Know—

If baseball excellence runs in the Griffey blood? It would certainly seem that way, as Griffey's father, Ken Sr., played for 19 seasons in the majors, and Griffey's brother, Craig, plays in the Cincinnati Reds organization. Do you think teams will be waiting to draft Griffey's son, Trey, when he graduates from high school in 2012?

Ken Griffey Jr.
c/o Seattle Mariners
P.O. Box 4100
83 King St.
Seattle, WA 98104

Yolanda Griffith

Power Forward, Chicago expansion team

∎ ∎ ∎ ∎ ∎ ∎ ∎ ∎ ∎ ∎ ∎ ∎ ∎ ∎ ∎ ∎

*W*hen Griffith joined the Long Beach StingRays, an expansion team, for the 1997–98 season, no one was sure how much of an impact she would make on the American Basketball League (ABL). Yolanda had been one of the top players in Europe for the past six seasons, but how would she do when she got back to the United States? All of those questions were put to rest as Griffith led the StingRays to the ABL Championship series in 1998. At the end of the season, Griffith was traded to a yet-to-be-named expansion team in her hometown, Chicago, where she hopes to have a similar impact. Don't bet against her.

So You Want to Know—

How Yolanda combines fun and work? Griffith took advantage of her love for video games when she agreed to participate in the making of the first women's pro basketball video game. She and Seattle Reign guard Kate Starbird served as models for the game.

Cool Credits

➤ NCAA all-American at Florida Atlantic University, 1993
➤ Played professionally in Germany, 1994–96
➤ Selected by the StingRays with the No. 1 pick in the ABL draft, 1997
➤ ABL Defensive Player of the Year, 1998
➤ ABL all-star, 1998
➤ Runner-up for ABL MVP, 1998
➤ Traded to the ABL Chicago expansion franchise, 1998

Vital Stats

➤ Height: 6'4"
➤ Weight: 180
➤ Birthplace: Chicago, Illinois
➤ Current residence: Chicago, Illinois

➤ Favorite food: Italian
➤ Hobbies: cooking and video games
➤ Nickname: Yo
➤ Favorite athlete: Scottie Pippen
➤ Family ties: a 9-year-old daughter, Candace

Yolanda Griffith
322 S. Green St., Suite 208
Chicago, IL 60661

Mia Hamm

Forward, U.S. Soccer Team

□ □ □ □ □ □ □ □ □ □ □ □ □ □ □ □ □ □ □

Over the past decade, Hamm has established herself as the best women's soccer player in the world. She has dominated the game ever since she started playing. Now Hamm is also a pioneer, as she is helping to start the first women's professional soccer league in the United States. In addition to being the most popular player—male or female—in the world, Mia has likewise contributed to the increasing popularity of women's soccer in America.

Birthday Beat
May 17, 1972

So You Want to Know—
How much more of an impact Mia is going to have on women's soccer? A lot. The United States hosts the women's World Cup in 1999, and after that a women's professional league is scheduled to be launched. Hamm is going to play for the United States in the World Cup, and her involvement in the professional league will give fans around the country a chance to see more of their favorite player.

Cool Credits

➤ Youngest player ever on the national team at the age of 15, 1987
➤ All-American at the University of North Carolina (UNC), 1990–93
➤ Led UNC to National Championships, 1990–1993
➤ NCAA Player of the Year, 1990, 1992, 1993
➤ U.S. Soccer Athlete of the Year, 1993–97 (only athlete to have won this four years in a row)
➤ Led U.S. to Olympic gold medal, 1996

Vital Stats

➤ Height: 5'3"
➤ Weight: 105
➤ Birthplace: Selma, Alabama
➤ Current residence: Chapel Hill, North Carolina

Mia Hamm
c/o U.S. Soccer Federation
1801-11 S. Prairie Ave.
Chicago, IL 60616

Dominik Hasek

Goalie, Buffalo Sabres

▼▼▼▼▼▼▼▼▼▼▼▼▼▼▼▼▼▼▼▼▼

Few players have ever come close to having the kind of year Hasek had in 1998. After entering the season with the best goals against average among active players, Hasek won his second Hart trophy, given to the league MVP. But it was in the Olympics that Dominik showed what he was truly capable of when he led the underdog Czech Republic past the United States, Canada, Russia, and Finland to win the gold medal. After the Olympics, Hasek was given a hero's welcome in Prague: 700,000 fans turned up at the airport to greet the arriving hockey team.

Vital Stats

➤ Height: 5'11"
➤ Weight: 168
➤ Birthplace: Pardubice, Czech Republic
➤ Current residence: Prague, Czech Republic
➤ Nickname: The Dominator
➤ Family ties: a brother who plays professional soccer in Europe
➤ Favorite food: pizza
➤ Favorite hockey player: Jaromir Jagr of the Pittsburgh Penguins

Cool Credits

➤ Drafted by the Chicago Blackhawks, 1988
➤ NHL all-star, 1993–98
➤ Vezina trophy winner, 1994, 1995, 1997, 1998
➤ Hart trophy winner, 1997, 1998
➤ Won Olympic gold medal, 1998

So You Want to Know—

How much the Czech Republic loves Hasek? The country's obsession with Dominik is pretty intense. When a world-famous astronomer discovered a huge comet more than 240 million miles away from the earth, he christened it the Dominik Hasek Comet.

Dominik Hasek
c/o Buffalo Sabres
Marine Midland Arena
One Seymour H. Knox III Plaza
Buffalo, NY 14203

Martina Hingis

Tennis Player

■ ■ ■ ■ ■ ■ ■ ■ ■ ■ ■ ■ ■ ■ ■ ■

Cool Credits

➤ Won U.S. Open, 1997
➤ Won Wimbledon, 1997
➤ Won Australian Open, 1997, 1998
➤ No. 1 player in the world, 1997, 1998

Vital Stats

➤ Height: 5'6"
➤ Weight: 115
➤ Birthplace: Košice, Slovakia
➤ Current residence: Trübbach, Switzerland
➤ Favorite movie: *Forrest Gump*
➤ Favorite singer: Jon Bon Jovi
➤ Favorite food: chicken fajitas

Birthday Beat
September 30, 1980

*A*t just 17 years of age, Hingis has already done more in two years on the women's tennis tour than most players do in an entire career. In 1997, Martina skyrocketed up the women's rankings as she won three of the four Grand Slam tournaments—Wimbledon, the U.S. Open, and the Australian Open—and secured her place as the best women's tennis player in the world. Hingis has given an incredible boost to tennis's popularity; thousands of fans flock to see her whenever she plays.

So You Want to Know—
If Hingis's parents predicted tennis greatness for their daughter? Perhaps. Hingis was named after another tennis great—Martina Navratilova.

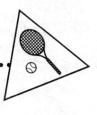

Martina Hingis
c/o Corel WTA Tour
1266 E. Main St., 4th Floor
Stamford, CT 06902

Michael Jordan

Shooting Guard, Chicago Bulls

Cool Credits

➤ Led University of North Carolina (UNC) at Chapel Hill to the NCAA Championships, 1982
➤ NCAA Player of the Year at UNC, 1984
➤ Led U.S. Olympic Team to the gold medal, 1984, 1992
➤ Selected by the Bulls with the third pick in the NBA draft, 1984
➤ Rookie of the Year, 1985
➤ NBA all-star, 1985, 1987–93, 1996–98
➤ Led NBA in scoring 1987–93, 1996–98
➤ Defensive Player of the Year, 1988
➤ NBA MVP, 1988, 1991, 1992, 1996, 1998
➤ Selected as one of the top 50 players in NBA history

Vital Stats

➤ Height: 6'6"
➤ Weight: 228
➤ Birthplace: Brooklyn, New York
➤ Current residence: Chicago, Illinois
➤ Favorite food: hamburgers
➤ Favorite athlete: Tiger Woods
➤ Nickname: Air

So You Want to Know—

If Jordan is a little looney? He was in 1996, when he joined forces with Looney Tunes characters Bugs Bunny, Porky Pig, Sylvester, Tweety Bird, and company to make the feature film *Space Jam*, which was a tremendous success. When asked why he decided to make the film, Jordan said, "I've always been a huge fan of Bugs Bunny. How could I possibly turn down the chance to work with him?"

Few would argue that Jordan is the best player in basketball. Since joining the NBA in 1984, His Royal Airness has led the Bulls to six NBA titles as of 1998. If anyone questions the impact he has had on the Bulls, all one has to do is look at the past seven seasons. The 1994 and 1995 championships, which the Bulls didn't win, took place when Jordan briefly retired from basketball to play professional baseball. Listing Michael's on-court accomplishments would take more pages than this entire book contains, but off the court Jordan is an absolute class act. Despite being one of the most famous people in the world, he still finds time to do charity work, make public appearances, and work with children.

Birthday Beat

February 17, 1963

Michael Jordan
c/o Chicago Bulls
1901 W. Madison St.
Chicago, IL 60612

Anna Kournikova

Tennis Player

▼▼▼▼▼▼▼▼▼▼▼▼▼▼▼▼▼▼

K ournikova has been groomed for stardom since she was 12 years old. It was at that age that she came to the United States to train at Nick Bollettieri's camp, where such players as Andrew Agassi, Jim Courier, and Pete Sampras got their start. Kournikova turned pro at 14, but the World Tennis Association (WTA) rules limited the number of matches she could play. That didn't stop her from making a huge impact, as she proved in 1997 by qualifying for the semifinals at Wimbledon. Anna has an on-court rivalry with Martina Hingis, the world's No. 1 player, that may keep tennis fans flocking to matches for years to come.

Birthday Beat
June 7, 1981

Cool Credits

➤ Top-ranked junior player in the world, 1995
➤ Won ITF Championships, 1996
➤ Qualified for the semifinals at Wimbledon, 1997
➤ Finalist at the Lipton Championships, 1998

Vital Stats

➤ Height: 5'6"
➤ Weight: 112
➤ Birthplace: Moscow, Russia
➤ Current residence: Bradenton, Florida
➤ Favorite athlete: Sergei Fedorov
➤ Favorite tennis players: Steffi Graf and Monica Seles
➤ Hobbies: shopping, listening to music, and watching hockey

So You Want to Know—

How famous tennis has made Anna? After the 1997 U.S. Open, Kournikova made her U.S. television debut on *The Tonight Show with Jay Leno*. Hopefully it won't be the last, as Anna plans to become an actress when her tennis career is over.

Anna Kournikova
c/o Bollettieri Sports Academy
5500 34th St. West
Bradenton, FL 34210

Michelle Kwan

Figure Skater

■ ■ ■ ■ ■ ■ ■ ■ ■ ■ ■ ■

Kwan let the world know she had arrived in 1994 when, at the age of 13, she played third fiddle to Olympians Nancy Kerrigan and Tonya Harding. While those two battled, Kwan quietly emerged as one of the world's best skaters. After winning the World Championships in 1996 and 1998, Michelle was favored to bring home a gold medal at the 1998 Olympics in Nagano, Japan. She won the silver, finishing a close second to rival American Tara Lipinski. Kwan will compete again for the United States at the Winter Olympics in 2002 in Salt Lake City, Utah.

Cool Credits

➤ Won silver medal at U.S. Championships, 1995, 1996
➤ World Champion, 1996, 1998

➤ Won silver medal at World Championships, 1997
➤ Olympic silver medalist, 1998
➤ National Champion, 1998

Vital Stats

➤ Height: 5'3"
➤ Weight: 102
➤ Birthplace: Torrance, California
➤ Current residence: Torrance, California
➤ Nickname: Shelly
➤ Favorite actors: Arnold Schwarzenegger and Sylvester Stallone

So You Want to Know—

If Kwan was gracious in defeat at the 1998 Olympics? She sure was. Despite her rivalry with Tara Lipinski, Kwan responded with class. When Lipinski won, Michelle said, "If I couldn't have won, I would have wanted her to." Or, as she told Jay Leno on the *Tonight Show* after returning from Japan, "I didn't lose the gold, I won the silver."

Michelle Kwan
c/o Ice Castle
P.O. Box 939480
Cottage Grove Rd.
Lake Arrowhead, CA 92352
or
Michelle Kwan
c/o Proper Marketing Association
44450 Pine Tree Dr., Suite 103
Plymouth, MI 48170

Justin Leonard

Golfer

□ □ □ □ □ □ □ □ □ □ □ □ □ □ □ □ □

If Tiger Woods is the best young player in golf, Leonard is a close second. He joined the PGA Tour immediately after graduating from the University of Texas in 1994 and has been climbing his way up the PGA ladder ever since. Although Justin may have been an unknown to all but the biggest golf fans for his first three years on the tour, that changed in 1997 when he won the British Open.

Birthday Beat
June 15, 1972

Cool Credits
➤ U.S. Amateur Champion, 1992
➤ All-American at University of Texas, 1993–94
➤ Won Buick Open, 1996
➤ Won British Open and Kemper Open, 1997
➤ Finished second at the PGA Championships, 1997

Vital Stats

➤ Height: 5'9"
➤ Weight: 160
➤ Birthplace: Dallas, Texas
➤ Current residence: Dallas, Texas, and Kiawah Island, South Carolina
➤ Favorite music: country
➤ Favorite food: Mexican
➤ Hobby: fishing

So You Want to Know—

What was the best moment of Leonard's career? Justin says winning the British Open in 1997 was the best, but only because of what happened afterward. A few weeks later he was invited to go onstage at a Garth Brooks concert. Leonard, a huge Brooks fan, graciously accepted.

Justin Leonard
c/o PGA Tour
112 PGA Tour Blvd.
Ponte Vedra Beach, FL 32082

Tara Lipinski

Figure Skater

Vital Stats

➤ Height: 4'11"
➤ Weight: 82
➤ Birthplace: Philadelphia, Pennsylvania
➤ Current residence: Sugarland, Texas
➤ Favorite movie: *Fools Rush In*
➤ Favorite TV show: *Party of Five*
➤ Favorite actress: Lacey Chabert
➤ Favorite actor: Tom Cruise
➤ Favorite athlete: Olympic gymnast Dominique Moceanu

Cool Credits

➤ World Champion, 1997
➤ U.S. Champion, 1997, 1998
➤ Won Olympic gold medal, 1998
➤ Turned pro, 1998
➤ Won Skate, Rattle and Roll Championships, 1998

So You Want to Know—

How much longer Tara plans to skate? "As long as it still feels good," she replies. But she wants to attend college and study to become an attorney, so fans had better enjoy her while they still can. There's no real rush, though; Lipinski is still only in high school.

Birthday Beat

June 10, 1982

When Lipinski won the gold medal at the 1998 Winter Olympics in Nagano, Japan, she joined an elite group of American figure skaters. Immediately afterward, people started talking about a repeat performance in 2002. But having done all she could as an amateur, Tara turned pro at the ripe old age of 15. Now she's skating on the pro circuit against Olympic medalists Nancy Kerrigan, Kristi Yamaguchi, and Debi Thomas. Not bad for someone who's not yet old enough to get her driver's license!

Tara Lipinski
c/o Detroit Skating Club
888 Dennison Ct.
Bloomfield Hills, MI 48302
http://www.taralipinski.com

Kenny Lofton

Outfielder, Cleveland Indians

■ ■ ■ ■ ■ ■ ■ ■ ■ ■ ■ ■ ■ ■ ■

After playing five seasons for the Cleveland Indians, Lofton was surprised and disappointed to hear that he'd been traded to the Atlanta Braves before the 1997 season. Lofton made the best of it, leading the Braves to the Eastern Division Championships. But when he became a free agent after the season ended, Lofton went back to Cleveland. The Indians are pretty lucky because Kenny is the most feared base stealer and one of the best centerfielders in the game.

So You Want to Know—

How good an athlete Lofton is? When he was attending the University of Arizona, Kenny played basketball as well as baseball. He was a teammate of Chicago Bulls' guard Steve Kerr and helped lead Arizona to the 1988 NCAA Final Four.

Birthday Beat

May 31, 1967

Cool Credits

➤ Picked by the Houston
Astros in the 1989
baseball draft
➤ Led American League
in stolen bases, 1992–96
➤ All-star, 1993–97
➤ Gold Glove winner,
1993–97
➤ Led American
League in triples
with 13, 1995

Vital Stats

➤ Height: 6'
➤ Weight: 180
➤ Birthplace: East
Chicago, Indiana
➤ Current residence:
Tucson, Arizona
➤ Favorite food:
Mexican
➤ Favorite athlete:
Michael Jordan

Kenny Lofton
c/o Cleveland Indians
2401 Ontario St.
Cleveland, OH 44115

Peyton Manning

Quarterback, Indianapolis Colts

▢ ▢ ▢ ▢ ▢ ▢ ▢ ▢ ▢ ▢ ▢ ▢ ▢ ▢ ▢ ▢ ▢ ▢ ▢

When the Colts picked Manning with the first selection in the 1998 NFL draft, fans across the country knew the team would improve. Manning is one of the best quarterbacks to come out of college in the past two decades. He has already been compared with such greats as John Elway, Steve Young, and Brett Favre. If his collegiate career at the University of Tennessee is any indication of what his pro career is going to be like, the Colts will be a force to be reckoned with.

Birthday Beat
March 4, 1976

□ □ □ □ □ □ □ □ □ □ □ □ □ □ □ □ □ □

Cool Credits

➤ National High School Player of the Year, 1993
➤ NCAA all-American, 1996, 1997
➤ Graduated from the University of Tennessee, 1997, where he holds virtually every passing record
➤ Sullivan Award Winner (given to nation's best amateur athlete), 1997
➤ Runner-up for the Heisman trophy, 1997

➤ Selected by the Colts with the first pick in the 1998 NFL draft

Vital Stats

➤ Height: 6'5"
➤ Weight: 228
➤ Birthplace: New Orleans, Louisiana
➤ Favorite food: Cajun
➤ Family ties: father is former New Orleans Saints quarterback Archie Manning

So You Want to Know—

How Manning has dealt with fame? Even while at Tennessee, Peyton was the state's biggest sports superstar. He was quick to give everything he could back to the community by reading stories to grade school students, making public appearances to help charities, and being a good role model for children.

Peyton Manning
c/o Indianapolis Colts
P.O. Box 535000
Indianapolis, IN 46253

Curtis Martin

Running Back, New York Jets

▼▼▼▼▼▼▼▼▼▼▼▼▼▼▼▼▼▼▼

Coming out of the University of Pittsburgh in 1995, Martin was virtually unknown. But during his first game in the NFL with the New England Patriots, he rushed for more than 100 yards and got two touchdowns, and he hasn't stopped running since. An all-pro selection every year he's been in the league, Curtis is one of an elite group of running backs to rush for more than 1,000 yards in his first three seasons. After signing with the Jets in the off-season, Martin was reunited with former coach Bill Parcells. It's safe to say that Martin will be as dominant a Jet as he was a Patriot.

52

Birthday Beat
May 1, 1973

Cool Credits

➤ All-Big East at the University of Pittsburgh, 1993, 1994
➤ NFL Rookie of the Year, 1995
➤ All-pro, 1995–97
➤ Rushed for more than 1,000 yards, 1995–97
➤ Led the New England Patriots to the Super Bowl, 1997
➤ Signed with the Jets as a free agent, 1998

Vital Stats

➤ Height: 5'11"
➤ Weight: 203
➤ Birthplace: Pittsburgh, Pennsylvania
➤ Current residence: New York, New York

So You Want to Know—

If Martin keeps his promises? He promised his mother that he would get his college degree at the University of Pittsburgh. When Martin joined the NFL in 1995, he was still a few courses short of graduating, but he attended summer school in 1996 and soon earned his degree in physical education.

Curtis Martin
c/o New York Jets
1000 Fulton Ave.
Hempstead, NY 11550

Pedro Martinez

Pitcher, Boston Red Sox

■ ■ ■ ■ ■ ■ ■ ■ ■ ■ ■ ■ ■ ■ ■

*I*n 1997, Martinez was the first pitcher in 25 years to strike out more than 300 batters and have an Earned Run Average under 2.00. That made him one of the most dominant pitchers in major-league baseball. Montreal Expos fans were no doubt surprised when Martinez was dealt to the Red Sox. In any uniform, though, Pedro is an excellent pitcher and is off to a hot start with Boston in 1998.

So You Want to Know—

If good pitching runs in the family? When someone looks at the Martinez family, they probably mutter, "Oh, brother!" That's because there are three Martinez brothers in the major leagues. In addition to Pedro, Ramon pitches for the Los Angeles Dodgers, and Jesus pitches for the Florida Marlins.

Birthday Beat
October 25, 1971

Vital Stats
➤ Height: 5'11"
➤ Weight: 170
➤ Birthplace: Manoguayabo, Dominican Republic
➤ Current residence: Santo Domingo, Dominican Republic
➤ Hobbies: swimming, reading, and listening to music
➤ Favorite food: Mexican

Cool Credits

➤ All-star, 1996, 1997
➤ Led the National League with a 1.90 Earned Run Average, 1997
➤ Became 14th player in history to strike out 300 batters in a season when he struck out 305, 1997

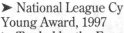

➤ National League Cy Young Award, 1997
➤ Traded by the Expos to the Red Sox for pitcher Carl Pavano, 1997

Pedro Martinez
c/o Boston Red Sox
Four Yawkey Way
Boston, MA 02215-3496

Brian McBride

Forward, Columbus Crew

□ □ □ □ □ □ □ □ □ □ □ □ □ □ □ □

McBride may not be as well known as some of his Major League Soccer (MLS) counterparts such as Alexi Lalas and Cobi Jones, but he is as feared as any. A member of the national team, he will be key to the United States' chances of winning the 1998 World Cup. Whenever McBride is on the field, the goalies pay close attention to where he is at all times. One look away, and Brian just might score a goal.

Vital Stats

➤ Height: 6'1"
➤ Weight: 170
➤ Birthplace: Arlington Heights, Illinois
➤ Current residence: Arlington Heights, Illinois
➤ Nickname: Bake
➤ Favorite athlete: Chris Chelios of the Chicago Blackhawks

Cool Credits

➤ NCAA all-American at St. Louis University, 1992, 1993
➤ NCAA Player of the Year, 1993
➤ Selected by the Crew with the first pick in the MLS draft, 1996
➤ Led the Crew to the playoffs, 1996, 1997
➤ U.S. National Team member, 1996–98
➤ Representing the United States at the 1998 World Cup

Birthday Beat
June 19, 1972

So You Want to Know—

If soccer is a risky enough sport for McBride? Apparently not. The admitted daredevil's favorite hobby is skydiving, which he engages in whenever he doesn't have any soccer commitments. What a schedule!

Brian McBride
c/o Columbus Crew
77 E. Nationwide Blvd.
Columbus, OH 43215

Mark McGwire

First Baseman, St. Louis Cardinals

▼▼▼▼▼▼▼▼▼▼▼▼▼▼▼▼▼▼▼▼

Vital Stats

➤ Height: 6'5"
➤ Weight: 250
➤ Birthplace: Pomona, California
➤ Current residence: Long Beach, California
➤ Family ties: a 9-year-old son, Matthew; brother Dan, who played in the NFL for the Miami Dolphins and the Seattle Seahawks
➤ Hobbies: playing golf and pool

Cool Credits

➤ Attended the University of Southern California
➤ Member of the 1984 Olympic Team
➤ College Player of the Year, 1984
➤ Selected by the Oakland A's in the first round of the 1984 baseball draft
➤ Rookie of the Year, 1987
➤ Set record for home runs by a rookie with 49, 1987
➤ Led the American League in home runs, 1987, 1996
➤ Won World Series with the Oakland A's, 1989
➤ American League all-star, 1987–92, 1995–97
➤ Second player to hit more than 50 home runs in consecutive seasons, 1996, 1997
➤ Led majors in home runs with 58, 1997
➤ *Sporting News* Man of the Year, 1997

Birthday Beat
October 1, 1963

He can rip the cover off a baseball with his bat. Literally. McGwire has been one of the most feared sluggers in baseball since he broke into the major leagues in 1987. In 1997, McGwire hit a total of 58 home runs with the Oakland A's and the Cardinals, to whom he was traded mid-season. Mark is such a powerful hitter that most pitchers would rather walk him than give him a chance to knock a pitch 500 feet!

So You Want to Know—

Just how much McGwire gives back to the community? Mark started the Mark McGwire Foundation in 1997 and plans to give a million dollars each season to help children across the country who have suffered from child abuse.

Mark McGwire
c/o St. Louis Cardinals
250 Stadium Plaza
St. Louis, MO 63102

Mike Modano

Center, Dallas Stars

■ ■ ■ ■ ■ ■ ■ ■ ■ ■ ■ ■ ■ ■ ■

When the Stars won the Presidents' Cup in 1998 for the best record in the NHL, it was easy to point to Modano as the reason. He is arguably the best American in the NHL and led the U.S. Hockey Team in the 1998 Olympics. Since breaking into the league in 1989, Mike has been a scoring force, and he shows no signs of letting up anytime soon.

Cool Credits

➤ Selected by the Stars with the first pick in the 1988 NHL draft
➤ Rookie of the Year, 1989–90
➤ NHL all-star, 1990–97
➤ Led the Stars to Stanley Cup Finals, 1991
➤ Helped lead Team USA to the gold medal at the Hockey World Cup, 1996

Vital Stats

➤ Height: 6'3"
➤ Weight: 200
➤ Birthplace: Livonia, Michigan
➤ Current residence: Dallas, Texas
➤ Hobby: Golf

Birthday Beat
June 7, 1970

Mike Modano
c/o Dallas Stars
c/o Reunion Arena
777 Sports St.
Dallas, TX 75207

Cristen Powell

Race Car Driver

▱ ▱ ▱ ▱ ▱ ▱ ▱ ▱ ▱ ▱ ▱ ▱ ▱ ▱ ▱ ▱ ▱ ▱

Even before she could legally get her driver's license, Powell was already turning heads on the National Hot Rod Association (NHRA) drag racing circuit. At the age of 13, Cristen won the 1992 U.S. National Championships, competing against drivers twice her age. In 1995, at the age of 16, Powell set a world record by reaching 241 miles per hour to take the No. 1 qualifying spot at the Sears Craftsman Nationals. She was the first and only woman ever to reach a speed that high. Powell set out to blaze a new trail by competing against the best drivers in the world—male and female. She's held her own and has won several races.

> **So You Want to Know—**
> How Powell celebrated her first professional win at the Mopar Auto Parts Nationals in New Jersey? She immediately flew back to Portland to attend her senior prom!

Cool Credits

➤ Attends Linfield College in Oregon
➤ Youngest female racer on the NHRA circuit
➤ Won U.S. National Championships, 1995
➤ Won Mopar Auto Parts Nationals, 1997
➤ Had fastest time of her career at 307.27 miles per hour at the Revell Nationals, 1997

Vital Stats

➤ Height: 5'6"
➤ Weight: 120
➤ Birthplace: Portland, Oregon
➤ Current residence: Portland, Oregon

➤ Favorite color: purple (her car is purple, and she races for the Royal Purple team)
➤ Nickname: The Little Princess
➤ Favorite music: country

Cristen Powell
c/o National Hot Rod Association
2035 Financial Way
Glendora, CA 91741
http://www.cristenpowell.com

Predrag "Preki" Radosavljevic

Midfielder, Kansas City Wizards

▼▼▼▼▼▼▼▼▼▼▼▼▼▼▼▼▼▼▼▼

*A*fter arriving in the United States in 1985, Preki quickly established himself as one of the best soccer players in the country. When the United States started its professional league, Major League Soccer (MLS), in 1996, Preki joined Kansas City and has been the strongest player in the league for the past three seasons. Preki became a U.S. citizen in 1996, and he represented the United States at the 1998 World Cup in France.

Birthday Beat
June 24, 1963

▼▼▼▼▼▼▼▼▼▼▼▼▼▼▼▼▼▼▼

Cool Credits

➤ Selected by the Wizards with the fourth overall pick in the 1996 MLS draft
➤ MLS all-star, 1996–98
➤ MLS MVP, 1997
➤ MLS Scoring Champion with 41 points, 1997
➤ All-time MLS leading scorer
➤ All-MLS First Team, 1996, 1997
➤ Playing for the U.S. at the 1998 World Cup

Vital Stats

➤ Height: 5'9"
➤ Weight: 165
➤ Birthplace: Belgrade, Yugoslavia
➤ Current residence: Kansas City, Missouri
➤ Family ties: a wife, Trish, and two kids, Nikola and Natasha

---

So You Want to Know—

How Preki got his nickname? After Radosavljevic came to the United States, Americans found it difficult to pronounce his last name, so a soccer coach gave him the nickname Preki, and it stuck.

Predrag "Preki" Radosavljevic
c/o Kansas City Wizards
706 Broadway St., Suite 100
Kansas City, MO 64105-2300

Ivan Rodriguez

Catcher, Texas Rangers

*I*n major-league baseball, most catchers are either hitters or fielders, but they can rarely handle both duties. Rodriguez is a notable exception. While playing the most demanding position in baseball, Rodriguez still hits for average and power, making him one of the most valuable catchers in the game.

Birthday Beat

November 30, 1971

Cool Credits

➤ Signed with the Rangers in 1988 at the age of 16

➤ Youngest player in the league for two seasons, 1991, 1992

➤ Won six Gold Gloves as the best fielder at his position, 1992–97

➤ Major-league all-star, 1992–97

➤ Won four Silver Slugger awards as the best hitter at his position, 1994–97

➤ Holds the major-league record for doubles by a catcher during a season with 47, 1996

Vital Stats

➤ Height: 5'9"

➤ Weight: 205

➤ Birthplace: Vega Baja, Puerto Rico

➤ Current residence: Rio Piedras, Puerto Rico

➤ Nickname: Pudge or IRod

➤ Family ties: a 6-year-old son, Ivan, and a 3-year-old daughter, Amanda

So You Want to Know—

How Ivan celebrated being promoted to the major leagues? On June 20, 1991, when he was called up to join the Rangers, Rodriguez made another big move: He married his longtime girlfriend, Maribel.

Ivan Rodriguez
c/o Texas Rangers
1000 Ballpark Way
Arlington, TX 76011

Patrick Roy

Goalie, Colorado Avalanche

I f you asked young goalies in the NHL who their idol was while they were growing up, most would say Patrick Roy. Arguably the best goalie in NHL history, Roy is a national hero in Canada, where he led the Montreal Canadiens to the Stanley Cup in 1986 and 1993. He was traded to the Colorado Avalanche in 1995 and immediately proved his worth, as the Avalanche won the Stanley Cup that season. Any team that has Roy is likely to be a winner.

So You Want to Know—

What Roy does for fun? He collects sports cards. Patrick has more than 85,000 in his collection, and his oldest card dates back to 1911.

Cool Credits

➤ Conn Smythe winner (playoff MVP), 1986, 1993
➤ Played for three Stanley Cup champion teams, 1986, 1993, 1996
➤ William M. Jennings trophy winner (fewest goals allowed), 1987–89, 1992
➤ Vezina trophy winner (league's best goalie), 1989, 1990, 1992
➤ Set an NHL record of 99 playoff wins
➤ NHL all-star, 1988, 1990–94, 1996, 1997
➤ Member of the 1998 Olympic Team

Vital Stats

➤ Height: 6'2"
➤ Weight: 192
➤ Birthplace: Quebec City, Quebec, Canada
➤ Current residence: Quebec City, Quebec, Canada
➤ Family ties: a wife, Michelle, and three children, Jonathon, Frederick, and Jana

Birthday Beat
October 5, 1965

Patrick Roy
c/o Colorado Avalanche
McNichols Sports Arena
1635 Clay St.
Denver, CO 80204-1799

Joe Sakic

Center, Colorado Avalanche

Vital Stats

➤ Height: 5'11"
➤ Weight: 185
➤ Birthplace: Burnaby, British Columbia, Canada
➤ Current residence: Denver, Colorado
➤ Family ties: a wife, Debbie, and a 1-year-old son, Mitchell
➤ Hobby: golf
➤ Favorite foods: lamb chops and Italian
➤ Favorite movie: *Scarface*
➤ Favorite musician: Garth Brooks

Cool Credits

➤ Selected by the Quebec Nordiques in the second round of the 1988 NHL draft
➤ NHL all-star, 1990–97
➤ Conn Smythe winner (playoff MVP), 1996
➤ Member of the Canadian Olympic Team, 1998

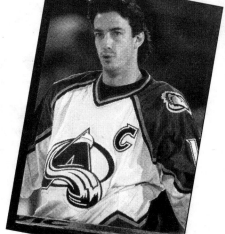

Birthday Beat

July 7, 1969

▼▼▼▼▼▼▼▼▼▼▼▼▼▼▼▼▼▼▼▼▼▼▼

*W*hile playing for the Quebec Nordiques from 1988 to 1994, Sakic was considered the best unknown player in the NHL. When the franchise moved to Colorado for the 1995–96 season, Joe became one of the best players in the NHL while leading Colorado to the 1996 Stanley Cup. With Sakic and teammate Peter Forsberg, Colorado has arguably the best centers in the NHL, and whenever Sakic is on the ice, you can bet goalies keep a sharp eye on him.

So You Want to Know—

What was the best moment of Sakic's illustrious career? He says it was when he skated on the ice holding the Stanley Cup after sweeping the Florida Panthers in 1996. By comparison, he says the best day of his life was the day his son, Mitchell, was born.

• •

Joe Sakic
c/o Colorado Avalanche
McNichols Sports Arena
1635 Clay St.
Denver, CO 80204-1799

• •

Barry Sanders
Running Back, Detroit Lions

■ ■ ■ ■ ■ ■ ■ ■ ■ ■ ■ ■ ■ ■

*S*anders is in a class all his own. After rushing for more than 2,000 yards during the 1997 NFL season, he left little doubt as to who has been the best running back in the league for the past decade. Barry has dominated the NFL ever since he was a rookie in 1989 and has continued to improve while other veteran runners grow closer to retirement. He holds the second highest career record for rushing yards and is closing in on the all-time record holder, Walter Payton.

Birthday Beat
July 16, 1968

■ ■ ■ ■ ■ ■ ■ ■ ■ ■ ■ ■ ■ ■ ■ ■

Cool Credits

➤ NCAA all-American at Oklahoma State University, 1988
➤ Heisman trophy winner, 1988
➤ Selected by the Lions with the third pick in the NFL draft, 1989
➤ Rookie of the Year, 1989
➤ Selected to Pro Bowl, 1989–97
➤ Holds NFL record for most consecutive 1,000 yard seasons, 1989–97
➤ Led NFC in rushing, 1989, 1990, 1994, 1996, 1997
➤ Led NFL in rushing, 1990, 1994, 1996, 1997
➤ NFL co-MVP, 1997

Vital Stats

➤ Height: 5'8"
➤ Weight: 203
➤ Birthplace: Wichita, Kansas
➤ Current residence: Detroit, Michigan

So You Want to Know—

If Sanders was a late bloomer? It appears so. While he was at Oklahoma State, Sanders didn't even win the starting running-back job until his senior season. Until that point, Barry was playing behind another running back, Thurman Thomas, whom he will probably join one day in the NFL Hall of Fame.

Barry Sanders
c/o Detroit Lions
1200 Featherstone Rd.
Pontiac, MI 48342

Curt Schilling

Pitcher, Philadelphia Phillies

▫ ▫ ▫ ▫ ▫ ▫ ▫ ▫ ▫ ▫ ▫ ▫ ▫ ▫ ▫ ▫

By striking out 319 players in 1997, Schilling established himself as one of the most feared pitchers in major-league baseball. It was a sweet comeback for a pitcher who had spent most of the 1996 season on the disabled list following shoulder surgery. Schilling hasn't cooled off much in 1998: He opened the season by beating Atlanta Braves ace Greg Maddux in back-to-back pitching duels. At 31 years of age, Curt is beginning to hit his prime. That's bad news for Phillies' opponents!

Birthday Beat
November 14, 1966

□ □ □ □ □ □ □ □ □ □ □ □ □ □ □ □ □ □ □

Cool Credits

➤ Selected by the Boston Red Sox in the second round of the 1986 baseball draft
➤ Played for the Baltimore Orioles and the Houston Astros before being traded to the Phillies in 1992
➤ National League all-star, 1997
➤ Led National League in strikeouts with 319 in 1997; was the 13th player in history to strike out more than 300 batters in a season

Vital Stats

➤ Height: 6'4"
➤ Weight: 228
➤ Birthplace: Anchorage, Alaska
➤ Current residence: Philadelphia, Pennsylvania
➤ Hobbies: golf and fishing
➤ Family ties: a 3-year-old son, Gehrig (named after Lou Gehrig), and a 1-year-old daughter, Gabriella

So You Want to Know—

What Schilling's favorite subject was in school? It was history, a subject that remains dear to him today. Curt spends his free time reading about World War II and collecting war memorabilia.

Curt Schilling
c/o Philadelphia Phillies
P.O. Box 7575
Philadelphia, PA 19101

Teemu Selanne

Right Wing, Mighty Ducks of Anaheim

▼▼▼▼▼▼▼▼▼▼▼▼▼▼▼▼▼▼▼

*A*fter an illustrious career playing junior-league hockey in Europe, Selanne arrived on the scene in the NHL in 1992 without the fanfare that accompanied many of his fellow players. He remained a quiet superstar for four seasons with the Winnipeg Jets. When Selanne was traded to the Mighty Ducks of Anaheim in 1996, his popularity soared, and he is now regarded as one of the best goal scorers in the league. With Teemu and teammate Paul Kariya in the line-up, the Ducks have one of the mightiest 1-2 punches in the NHL!

Cool Credits

➤ Picked by the Winnipeg Jets in the 1988 NHL draft
➤ Traded by the Jets to the Mighty Ducks in 1996 for Oleg Tverdosky
➤ Led NHL in points scored with 132, 1993
➤ NHL all-star, 1993–98
➤ Second in NHL in points scored with 109, 1997
➤ First Team all-NHL, 1997, 1998
➤ Played for the silver medal–winning Finland Olympic Team, 1998

Vital Stats

➤ Height: 6'0"
➤ Weight: 200
➤ Birthplace: Helsinki, Finland
➤ Current residence: Helsinki, Finland
➤ Nickname: The Flying Finn
➤ Family ties: a 2-year-old son, Eemil
➤ Favorite sport: auto racing
➤ Hobbies: fishing and playing with his two rottweilers

So You Want to Know—

How popular Selanne is in his homeland, Finland? When Teemu returns to Helsinki after each NHL season, a parade is held in his honor.

Birthday Beat

July 3, 1970

• • • • • • • • • • • • • • • • •

Teemu Selanne
c/o Mighty Ducks of Anaheim
Arrowhead Pond
2695 E. Katella Ave.
Anaheim, CA 92806

Annika Sorenstam

Golfer

■ ■ ■ ■ ■ ■ ■ ■ ■ ■ ■ ■ ■ ■ ■ ■ ■ ■

Cool Credits

➤ NCAA Player of the Year at the University of Arizona, 1991
➤ NCAA all-American, 1991, 1992
➤ LPGA Rookie of the Year, 1993
➤ Swedish Athlete of the Year, 1995
➤ Won U.S. Open, 1995, 1996
➤ No. 1 ranked player in the world, 1995–97
➤ Won LPGA Championship, 1997

Vital Stats

➤ Height: 5'6"
➤ Weight: 115
➤ Birthplace: Stockholm, Sweden
➤ Current residence: Stockholm, Sweden
➤ Hobby: cooking

Birthday Beat

October 9, 1970

So You Want to Know—

What was the best day of Sorenstam's career? That would be October 24, 1996, but it didn't have anything to do with winning a title. It was the day Annika's younger sister, Charlotta, joined the LPGA Tour.

■ ■ ■ ■ ■ ■ ■ ■ ■ ■ ■ ■ ■ ■ ■ ■

*A*fter winning a whopping six tournaments in 1997, Sorenstam proved she was the most dominant player on the Ladies Professional Golf Association (LPGA) Tour. Sorenstam finished the 1997 season as the top-ranked woman on the tour for the third year in a row and is well on her way to another title in 1998. At just 27 years of age, Annika should be wowing golf crowds for a long time to come.

Annika Sorenstam
c/o LPGA
100 International Golf Dr.
Daytona Beach, FL 32124-1092

Carlos Valderrama

Forward, Miami Fusion

☐ ☐ ☐ ☐ ☐ ☐ ☐ ☐ ☐ ☐ ☐ ☐ ☐ ☐ ☐ ☐ ☐

*I*n 1994, Valderrama became one of the most popular soccer players in the world. During the World Cup, no one could stop talking about him, and it wasn't only because of his frizzy shoulder-length hair. Carlos had been one of the top players in South America, but in 1996, when the United States launched Major League Soccer (MLS), he decided to come to America. He joined the Tampa Bay Mutiny and became one of the most celebrated players in the MLS almost overnight. Now with the Miami Fusion, Valderrama is still making opposing goalies shiver with his speed and acrobatics on the field.

Cool Credits

➤ Member of the Colombian World Cup team, 1990, 1994, 1998
➤ South American Player of the Year, 1992, 1994
➤ Captain of the Colombian National Team, 1993–98
➤ MLS MVP, 1996
➤ MLS all-star, 1996–98
➤ All-Star Game MVP, 1997

Vital Stats

➤ Height: 5'9"
➤ Weight: 161
➤ Birthplace: Santa Marta, Colombia
➤ Current residence: Santa Marta, Colombia
➤ Favorite movie: *The Bodyguard*
➤ Favorite food: seafood
➤ Favorite actor: Michael Douglas
➤ Favorite athlete: Michael Jordan

So You Want to Know—

Who Valderrama trusts to cut his world-famous hair? Stylists around the world have offered their services, but only one person, Carlos's wife, Claribeth, is ever allowed to touch his hair.

Birthday Beat

September 2, 1961

Carlos Valderrama
c/o Miami Fusion
2200 Commercial Blvd., Suite 104
Fort Lauderdale, FL 33309

Larry Walker
Outfielder, Colorado Rockies

Walker had one of the best seasons in National League history in 1997 when he batted .366, led the National League with 49 home runs, knocked in 130 RBIs, and stole 33 bases. He was the runaway winner in the National League MVP voting and is a major reason the Rockies are consistently one of the best-hitting teams in baseball.

So You Want to Know—
What Walker's favorite sport is? Surprisingly, it's not baseball. While growing up in Canada, where hockey is the national sport, Larry was a goalie in the junior leagues before discovering he was a better baseball player. Walker is still a regular at Colorado Avalanche games and was a junior-league teammate of former Boston Bruins player Cam Neely.

Birthday Beat
December 1, 1966

Cool Credits

➤ National League all-star, 1992, 1997
➤ Gold Glove winner, 1993, 1994, 1997
➤ Led National League in doubles with 44, 1994
➤ Led National League in home runs with 49, 1997
➤ National League MVP, 1997
➤ Silver Slugger winner, 1997

Vital Stats

➤ Height: 6'3"
➤ Weight: 235
➤ Birthplace: Maple Ridge, British Columbia, Canada
➤ Current residence: Aurora, Colorado
➤ Family ties: a 5-year-old daughter, Brittany Marie

Larry Walker
c/o Colorado Rockies
2001 Blake St.
Denver, CO 80205-2000

Venus Williams

Tennis Player

■ ■ ■ ■ ■ ■ ■ ■ ■ ■ ■ ■ ■ ■

Williams seemingly came out of nowhere in the fall of 1997, when she reached the finals of the U.S. Open before losing to Martina Hingis. Venus had been on the tennis circuit since the age of 14, but her father, who is also her coach, limited the number of matches she played so that she would be ready when she started playing full time. It proved to be a wise move, as she is one of the top rising stars on the tennis tour. After just a year of playing regularly, Venus is ranked in the top 10 and has her eye on No. 1.

Birthday Beat
June 17, 1980

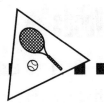

Cool Credits

➤ Turned pro, 1995
➤ Semifinalist at U.S. Open, 1997
➤ Won the IGA Tennis Classic, 1998
➤ Won Lipton Championships, 1998

Vital Stats

➤ Height: 5'11"
➤ Weight: 137
➤ Birthplace: Lynwood, California
➤ Current residence: Lynwood, California
➤ Hobbies: shopping and hanging out with her sister, Serena
➤ Favorite performer: actress/singer Brandy
➤ Favorite food: Mexican

So You Want to Know—

Where Venus is when she's not on the court? Probably having her hair done. The 18-year-old Williams is known for the many colorful beads she wears in her long braided hair. A hair salon session can take up to four hours when Venus changes her braids and beads.

Venus Williams
c/o Corel WTA tour
1266 E. Main St., 4th Floor
Stamford, CT 06902

Tiger Woods
Golfer

*T*he huge rise in popularity that golf has seen in the past two seasons can be directly tied to Tiger Woods. Not only is he one of the best young players on the PGA Tour, but he is also inspiring kids to take up golf and sparking an interest in a sport that was previously believed to appeal mostly to senior citizens. After having the most headline-grabbing career ever as an amateur, Woods turned pro in 1996 at the age of 20 and hasn't stopped turning heads since.

Cool Credits
➤ Attended Stanford University
➤ Won three U.S. Amateur Championships, 1994–96
➤ *Sports Illustrated*'s Sportsman of the Year, 1996
➤ PGA Rookie of the Year, 1996
➤ Won Las Vegas Invitational and Oldsmobile Classic, 1996

Birthday Beat
December 30, 1975

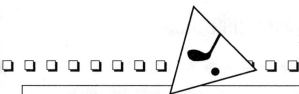

So You Want to Know—

How long Tiger has been dominant in golf? Practically ever since he learned to walk! Tiger started playing golf when he was only 1½ years old and showed a knack for it right away. At the age of 2, he appeared on *The Mike Douglas Show* and putted against Bob Hope. When he was 5, he was featured in *Golf Digest*. Is it any wonder his greatness has continued?

➤ Won Masters Championships, Mercedes Championships, Bryon Nelson Classic, Western Open, Pebble Beach Pro Am, World Series of Golf, MasterCard Colonial, Buick Open, and Bay Hill Invitational, 1997

➤ Led PGA money list, 1997

Vital Stats

➤ Height: 6'2"
➤ Weight: 160
➤ Birthplace: Cypress, California
➤ Current residence: Orlando, Florida
➤ Favorite athlete: Michael Jordan
➤ Favorite actor: Kevin Costner
➤ Hobbies: basketball and video games

Tiger Woods
c/o PGA Tour
112 PGA Tour Blvd.
Ponte Vedra Beach, FL 32082

Team Addresses

*I*f your favorite sports stars aren't featured in this book, you may be able to reach them through their teams. Here are addresses for most of the professional football, baseball, basketball, and hockey teams in the United States (and a few in Canada).

National Football League

Arizona Cardinals
P.O. Box 888
Phoenix, AZ 85001-0888

Atlanta Falcons
Atlanta Falcons Complex
One Falcon Place
Suwanee, GA 30174

Baltimore Ravens
11001 Owing Mills Blvd.
Owing Mills, MD 21117

Buffalo Bills
One Bills Drive
Orchard Park, NY 14127

Carolina Panthers
800 S. Mint St.
Charlotte, NC 28202-1502

Chicago Bears
Halas Hall
250 N. Washington Rd.
Lake Forest, IL 60045

Cincinnati Bengals
One Bengals Drive
Cincinnati, OH 45204

Dallas Cowboys
One Cowboys Parkway
Irving, TX 75063

Denver Broncos
13655 Broncos Pkwy.
Englewood, CO 80112

Detroit Lions
1200 Featherstone Rd.
Pontiac, MI 48342

Green Bay Packers
P.O. Box 10628
Green Bay, WI 54307-0628

Indianapolis Colts
P.O. Box 535000
Indianapolis, IN 46253

Jacksonville Jaguars
One Alltel Stadium Place
Jacksonville, FL 32202

Kansas City Chiefs
One Arrowhead Drive
Kansas City, MO 64129

Miami Dolphins
7500 SW 30th St.
Davie, FL 33314

Minnesota Vikings
9520 Viking Dr.
Eden Prairie, MN 55344

New England Patriots
60 Washington St.
Foxboro, MA 02035

New Orleans Saints
5800 Airline Hwy.
Metairie, LA 70003

New York Giants
Giants Stadium
East Rutherford, NJ 07073

New York Jets
1000 Fulton Ave.
Hempstead, NY 11550

Oakland Raiders
1220 Harbor Bay Pkwy.
Alameda, CA 94502

Philadelphia Eagles
3501 S. Broad St.
Philadelphia, PA 19148

Pittsburgh Steelers
300 Stadium Circle
Pittsburgh, PA 15212

St. Louis Rams
One Rams Way
St. Louis, MO 63045

San Diego Chargers
P.O. Box 609609
San Diego, CA 92160-9609

San Francisco 49ers
4949 Centennial Blvd.
Santa Clara, CA 95054-1229

Seattle Seahawks
11220 NE 53rd St.
Kirkland, WA 98033

Tampa Bay Buccaneers
One Buccaneer Place
Tampa, FL 33607

Tennessee Oilers
Baptist Sports Park
7640 Hwy. 70 South
Nashville, TN 37221

Washington Redskins
P.O. Box 17247
Dulles International Airport
Washington, DC 20041

National Basketball Association

Atlanta Hawks
One CNN Center, Suite 405
South Tower
Atlanta, GA 30303

Boston Celtics
151 Merrimac St.
Boston, MA 02114

Charlotte Hornets
100 Hive Dr.
Charlotte, NC 28217

Chicago Bulls
1901 W. Madison St.
Chicago, IL 60612

Cleveland Cavaliers
One Center Court
Cleveland, OH 44115-4001

Dallas Mavericks
777 Sports St.
Dallas, TX 75207

Denver Nuggets
1635 Clay St.
Denver, CO 80204

Detroit Pistons
Two Championship Drive
Auburn Hills, MI 48362

Golden State Warriors
7000 Coliseum Way
Oakland, CA 94621-1918

Houston Rockets
10 Greenway Plaza
Houston, TX 77046-3865

Indiana Pacers
300 E. Market St.
Indianapolis, IN 46204

Los Angeles Clippers
3939 S. Figueroa St.
Los Angeles, CA 90037

Los Angeles Lakers
3900 W. Manchester Blvd.
P.O. Box 10
Inglewood, CA 90306

Miami Heat
Miami Arena
Miami, FL 33136-4102

Milwaukee Bucks
1001 N. Fourth St.
Milwaukee, WI 53203-1312

Minnesota Timberwolves
600 First Ave. North
Minneapolis, MN 55403

New Jersey Nets
405 Murray Hill Pkwy.
East Rutherford, NJ
07073

New York Knicks
Two Pennsylvania Plaza
New York, NY 10121-0091

Orlando Magic
One Magic Place
Orlando Arena
Orlando, FL 32801

Philadelphia 76ers
Veterans Stadium
P.O. Box 25040
Philadelphia, PA 19147-
0240

Phoenix Suns
201 E. Jefferson
Phoenix, AZ 85004

Portland Trail Blazers
One Center Court, Suite
200
Portland, OR 97227

Sacramento Kings
One Sports Parkway
Sacramento, CA 95834

San Antonio Spurs
100 Montana St.
San Antonio, TX 78203-
1031

Seattle Supersonics
190 Queen Anne Ave.
North, Suite 200
Seattle, WA 98109-9711

Toronto Raptors
WaterPark Place
20 Bay St., Suite 1702
Toronto, Ontario M5J 2N8
Canada

Utah Jazz
301 W. South Temple
Salt Lake City, UT 84101

Vancouver Grizzlies
800 Griffiths Way
Vancouver, British
Columbia V6B 6G1
Canada

Washington Wizards
USAir Arena
Landover, MD 20785

Major League Baseball

Anaheim Angels
2000 Gene Autry Way
Anaheim, CA 92806

Arizona Diamondbacks
401 E. Jefferson
Phoenix, AZ 85003

Atlanta Braves
P.O. Box 4064
Atlanta, GA 30302

Baltimore Orioles
33 W. Camden St.
Baltimore, MD 21201

Boston Red Sox
Four Yawkey Way
Boston, MA 02215-3496

Chicago Cubs
1060 W. Addison St.
Chicago, IL 60613-4397

Chicago White Sox
333 W. 35th St.
Chicago, IL 60616

Cincinnati Reds
100 Cinergy Field
Cincinnati, OH 45202

Cleveland Indians
2401 Ontario St.
Cleveland, OH 44115

Colorado Rockies
2001 Blake St.
Denver, CO 80205-2000

Detroit Tigers
Tiger Stadium
Detroit, MI 48216

Florida Marlins
2267 NW 199th St.
Miami, FL 33056

Houston Astros
P.O. Box 288
Houston, TX 77001-0288

Kansas City Royals
Kauffman Stadium
P.O. Box 419969
Kansas City, MO 64141

Los Angeles Dodgers
1000 Elysian Park Ave.
Los Angeles, CA 90012

Milwaukee Brewers
County Stadium
P.O. Box 3099
Milwaukee, WI 53201-
3099

Minnesota Twins
34 Kirby Puckett Pl.
Minneapolis, MN 55415

Montreal Expos
4549 Pierre-de-Coubertin
Ave.
Montreal, Quebec H1V
1N7
Canada

New York Mets
123-10 Roosevelt Ave.
Flushing, NY 11368-1699

New York Yankees
Yankee Stadium
E. 161 St. and River Ave.
Bronx, NY 10451

Oakland A's
7677 Oakport St., Suite
200
Oakland, CA 94621

Philadelphia Phillies
P.O. Box 7575
Philadelphia, PA 19101

Pittsburgh Pirates
600 Stadium Circle
Pittsburgh, PA 15212

St. Louis Cardinals
250 Stadium Plaza
St. Louis, MO 63102

San Diego Padres
P.O. Box 2000
San Diego, CA 92112-
2000

San Francisco Giants
3Com Park at
Candlestick Park
San Francisco, CA 94124

Seattle Mariners
P.O. Box 4100
83 King St.
Seattle, WA 98104

Tampa Bay Devil Rays
One Tropicana Drive
St. Petersburg, FL 33705

Texas Rangers
1000 Ballpark Way
Arlington, TX 76011

Toronto Blue Jays
One Blue Jays Way, Suite
3200
Toronto, Ontario M5V 1J1
Canada

National Hockey League

Boston Bruins
One Fleet Center, Suite
250
Boston, MA 02114-1303

Buffalo Sabres
Marine Midland Arena
One Seymour H. Knox III
Plaza
Buffalo, NY 14203

Calgary Flames
P.O. Box 1540
Station M
Calgary, Alberta T2P 3B9
Canada

Carolina Hurricanes
5000 Aerial Center, Suite
100
Morrisville, NC 27560

Chicago Blackhawks
1901 W. Madison St.
Chicago, IL 60612

Colorado Avalanche
McNichols Sports Arena
1635 Clay St.
Denver, CO 80204-1799

Dallas Stars
211 Cowboys Pkwy.
Irving, TX 75063

Detroit Red Wings
600 Civic Center Dr.
Detroit, MI 48226

Edmonton Oilers
Edmonton Coliseum
Edmonton, Alberta T58
4M9
Canada

Florida Panthers
100 NE Third Ave., 2nd
Floor
Fort Lauderdale, FL
33301

Los Angeles Kings
3900 W. Manchester Blvd.
Inglewood, CA 90305

Mighty Ducks of Anaheim
Arrowhead Pond
2695 E. Katella Ave.
Anaheim, CA 92806

Montreal Canadiens
1260 rue de La
Gauchetiere Ouest
Montreal, Quebec H3B
5E8
Canada

New Jersey Devils
P.O. Box 504
East Rutherford, NJ 07073

New York Islanders
Nassau Veterans
Memorial Coliseum
Uniondale, NY 11553

New York Rangers
Two Pennsylvania Plaza
New York, NY 10121

Ottawa Senators
1000 Palladium Dr.
Kanata, Ontario K2V 1A5
Canada

Philadelphia Flyers
CoreStates Center
One CoreStates Complex
Philadelphia, PA 19148

Phoenix Coyotes
One Renaissance Square
Two N. Central, Suite 1930
Phoenix, AZ 85004

Pittsburgh Penguins
Civic Arena
66 Mario Lemieux Pl.
Pittsburgh, PA 15219

St. Louis Blues
Kiel Center
1401 Clark
St. Louis, MO 63103

San Jose Sharks
525 W. Santa Clara St.
San Jose, CA 95113

Tampa Bay Lightning
Ice Palace
401 Channels Dr.
Tampa, FL 33602

Toronto Maple Leafs
Maple Leaf Gardens
60 Carlton St.
Toronto, Ontario M5B
1L1
Canada

Vancouver Canucks
General Motors Place
800 Griffiths Way
Vancouver, British
Columbia V6B 6G1
Canada

Washington Capitals
US Airways Arena
One Harry S Truman
Drive
Landover, MD 20785

Photo Credits

Cover:
Tara Lipinski, Mike Powell; Tiger Woods,
David Cannon; Michael Jordan, John Cichici;
Mark McGwire, Jamie Squire

Interiors:
Brian Bahr: pp. 8, 15, 19, 21, 68, 70
Al Bello: p. 84
Clive Brunskill: pp. 40, 47
David Cannon: p. 86
John Cichici: p. 39
Glenn Cratty: p. 76
Stephen Dunn: p. 64
Jon Ferrey: p. 42
Otto Greule: p. 60
Scott Halleran: p. 22
Jed Jacobsohn: pp. 16, 52, 72, 83
Craig Jones: pp. 24, 79
Allen Kee: p. 80
Robert Laberge: p. 11
Vincent LaForet: p. 50
Andy Lyons: p. 31
Craig Melvin: pp. 12, 74
Doug Pensinger: p. 28
Cary Prior: p. 36
David Seelic: pp. 49, 55
Jamie Squire: pp. 44, 57, 59
Rick Stewart: pp. 27, 34, 66
Damian Strohmeyer: p. 33